Raccoons

Raccoons

Patrick Merrick

THE CHILD'S WORLD®, INC.

Library of Congress Cataloging-in-Publication Data
Merrick, Patrick.
Raccoons / by Patrick Merrick.
p.   cm.
Includes index.
Summary: Describes the physical characteristics,
behavior, habitat, and life cycle of raccoons.
ISBN 1-56766-504-7 (lib. reinforced : alk paper)
1. Raccoons—Juvenile literature.   [1. Raccoons.]   I. Title.
QL737.C26M47   1998
599.76'32—dc21   97-27835
CIP
AC

Photo Credits

© 1993 Barbara Gerlach/Dembinsky Photo Assoc. Inc: 16
© 1994 Barbara Gerlach/Dembinsky Photo Assoc. Inc: 13
© Charles Krebs/Tony Stone Images: 19
© Daniel J. Cox/Natural Exposures: cover, 2
© 1994 Doug Locke/Dembinsky Photo Assoc. Inc: 30
© Dwight R. Kuhn: 20, 23
© 1993 Gijsbert van Frankenhuyzen: 24
© 1993 Mike Barlow/Dembinsky Photo Assoc. Inc: 26
© Russ Kinne/Comstock, Inc.: 15
© Sharon Cummings/Dembinsky Photo Assoc. Inc: 9
© 1994 Skip Moody/Dembinsky Photo Assoc. Inc: 6
© Tom Tietz/Tony Stone Images: 29
© William Ervin/Comstock, Inc.:10

On the cover...

Front cover: These raccoons are climbing in a tree.
Page 2: This raccoon is playing in a hollow tree.

Table of Contents

It is a quiet summer evening. As you are getting ready for bed, you hear a noise outside. You look out and see that your trash cans have been tipped over! Garbage is thrown everywhere. In the morning, you go to investigate. All you see is little handprints in the dirt. What type of creature did this? It was probably one of our cutest and smartest animals—the raccoon.

⇐ A raccoon left these tracks in the sand near a stream.

What Do Raccoons Look Like?

Raccoons belong to a group of animals called **mammals**. Mammals have hair all over their bodies. They also have warm blood and feed their babies milk from their bodies. Cows, dogs, bears, and people are mammals, too.

This raccoon is watching other animals in a field. ⇒

Raccoons have small, fat bodies covered with thick, brownish gray fur. Most raccoons weigh about 15 pounds, but some can grow to over 50 pounds! They have long noses and ears that stick straight up. They also have long, striped tails. But most people know raccoons because of their black "masks." The mask is really just dark fur near the raccoon's eyes.

Where Do Raccoons Live?

Many animals can only live in one kind of place, or **environment**. An environment contains the type of land, plants, and water the animal needs to live. If that environment is destroyed, the animal dies. Raccoons, however, can live in many different environments. They are found in swamps, forests, meadows, beaches, and even cities!

This raccoon lives in a forest in Michigan. ⇒

Raccoons often make their homes, or **dens**, inside hollow trees. But if there are no trees handy, raccoons will live in haystacks, sheds, or even people's attics. Raccoons stay in one den for a while, then move to a different one.

This young raccoon made its den inside a hollow tree. ⇒

When the first winter snow comes, the raccoon lies down in its den and goes to sleep. It spends most of the winter inside, only coming out to eat during warmer weather. If it is a long, cold winter, the raccoon won't eat at all. The raccoon might lose up to half its weight before spring comes again.

What Do Raccoons Eat?

If you go looking for raccoons during the day, all you will find are their tracks. If you want to see a raccoon, you must look at night. That's because raccoons are **nocturnal**. Nocturnal animals rest during the day and are active after dark. At night, raccoons hunt for food.

Raccoons like this one are most active at night. ⇒

Raccoons are **omnivores**, which means that they eat plants as well as other animals. Raccoons are hungry all of the time. They will eat almost anything—even garbage! Mostly, though, they eat things like nuts, fruit, crayfish, frogs, worms, eggs, and fish.

How Do Raccoons Catch Their Food?

A raccoon uses its front paws to reach and climb and to grab the things it eats. These front paws are almost as useful as your hands. With its paws, a raccoon can crack open crayfish shells or even unlock food coolers! Raccoons are very smart animals. Before they eat, they like to bring their food to water. Scientists think the raccoons like to wash their food before they eat it.

This raccoon is using its paws to search for food in a pond. ⇒

How Are Baby Raccoons Born?

During January or February, a male and female raccoon mate. After mating, the male and female go back to their own dens. Nine weeks later, the female gives birth to about six baby raccoons. The baby raccoons, or **kits**, are very tiny. They are blind because their eyelids won't open yet. After about three weeks, their eyes open and the kits begin to move around. Now they can follow their mothers out into the night. When they are several months old, they go off to live on their own.

⇐ This kit is peeking out of its den during the day.

Do Raccoons Have Enemies?

Most raccoons live to be about 15 years old. That is because they don't have many natural enemies. Foxes, owls, and bobcats all eat baby raccoons. But when a raccoon is fully grown, few animals want to face its sharp teeth and claws.

The biggest danger to healthy raccoons is people. Some raccoons are hunted for their fur. Others are trapped by farmers who want to stop them from eating their crops. But even more raccoons die because they are hit by cars or trucks.

⇐ Bobcats like this one sometimes hunt raccoons for food.

Are Raccoons Dangerous?

Many people love raccoons. Some people even raise raccoon babies or try to keep them as pets. This is not a good idea! Raccoons are wild animals, and they do not make good pets when they grow up. It takes special training to learn how to raise babies so they will be healthy and able to return to the wild. Only people who have this special training should care for raccoons.

It is easy to see why people want to keep raccoons as pets. ⇒

The most dangerous problem with raccoons is the diseases they often carry. The best known is **rabies**, a disease that kills animals and people. Someone who is bitten by a raccoon with rabies can become very sick or even die. Because of this problem, you should never go near a wild raccoon. If you are ever bitten, wash the bite carefully and get to a doctor right away.

As long as we are careful, raccoons can be a joy to watch. With their cuddly looks and natural curiosity, they will always be one our most enjoyed animals.

← This young raccoon is peeking out from a hollow log.

Glossary

environment (en–VY–run–ment)
An animal's environment is the type of area in which it lives. Raccoons live in many types of environments.

dens (DENZ)
Dens are hollow spots in trees or in the ground where animals live. Raccoon dens are often in hollow trees.

kits (KITS)
A baby raccoon is called a kit. Kits live with their mothers for several months.

mammals (MA–mullz)
Mammals are animals that have hair and warm blood and feed their babies milk from their bodies. Raccoons, cows, dogs, and people are all mammals.

nocturnal (nok–TUR–null)
Nocturnal animals sleep during the day and are active only at night. Raccoons are nocturnal.

omnivore (OM–ni–vor)
An omnivore is an animal that eats both plants and other animals. Raccoons are omnivores.

rabies (RAY–beez)
Rabies is a very dangerous disease. Raccoons and other animals sometimes carry rabies.

Index